Each Day

&

Each Night

Each Day & Each Night

Celtic prayers from Iona

J. Philip Newell

WILD GOOSE PUBLICATIONS

First published 1994, reissued in a new edition 2003 and reprinted 2008 by
Wild Goose Publications
Fourth Floor, Savoy House, 140 Sauchiehall Street, Glasgow G2 3DH, UK
web: www.ionabooks.com
Wild Goose Publications is the publishing division of the Iona Community.
Scottish Charity No. SCO03794. Limited Company Reg. No. SCO96243.

ISBN 978-1-901557-69-5

Cover design © 2002 Wild Goose Publications

A catalogue record for this book is available from the British Library.

Overseas distribution
Australia: Willow Connection Pty Ltd, Unit 4A, 3-9 Kenneth Road, Manly Vale, NSW 2093
New Zealand: Pleroma, Higginson Street, Otane 4170, Central Hawkes Bay
Canada: Novalis Publishing & Distribution, 10 Lower Spadina Avenue, Suite 400, Toronto, Ontario M5V 2Z2

Produced by Reliance Production Company, Hong Kong
Printed and bound in China

Contents

PREFACE

This collection of morning and evening prayers (originally published in 1994) grew initially out of my desire for a discipline and shape in daily personal prayer. During my time as Warden of Iona Abbey, members and associates of the Iona Community, whose first rule is to pray and study the scriptures daily, expressed the need for a prayer book for individual use. I hope these prayers will continue to be helpful to them and to the many others who have made use of this resource well beyond the bounds of the Iona Community.

On Iona people often indicated to me that they would like their prayers at home to be based on the major themes of daily prayer at the Abbey, and so I wove the weekly pattern of themes from Iona into this six-day cycle of prayer. On Mondays the emphasis is on justice and peace; on Tuesdays there is a concentration on prayer for healing; on Wednesdays the focus is on the goodness of creation and care for the earth; on Thursdays the theme is commitment to Christ; on Fridays there is a celebration of the communion of heaven and earth; and on Saturdays the emphasis is on welcome and hospitality. Originally I assumed that on Sundays the norm was to join others for prayer rather than being on one's own. I continue to hope that this can be the pattern for our lives.

Included in the appendix is a lectionary of psalms and gospel readings used in the Abbey. This is based upon 'The Revised Common Lectionary' prepared by the Consultation on Common Texts (1978) in which many churches participated, including the Roman Catholic, Anglican, Presbyterian and Methodist.

The little island of Iona in the Western Isles of Scotland is known as one of Britain's most historic holy places. It was there in the 6th century that St Columba established his mission from Ireland. Iona is remembered as the cradle of Christianity for much of Scotland and northern England. It is a beautiful Hebridean island, described by George MacLeod – the founder of the modern-day Iona Community – as 'a thin place' in which matter is only thinly separated from spirit. This great Celtic mystic of the 20th century, Lord MacLeod of Fuinary, who was also a Church of Scotland minister, saw that the eternal is 'seeping' through the physical. He was not, of course, speaking only of Iona, but of Iona as a sign or sacrament of what is most deeply true of every place and every time. As the overlapping strands in Celtic artwork suggest, the life of heaven is inseparably woven into the life of earth. God is the Life within all life, the Light behind all light. 'Shafts of that divine light,' said the 4th-century Celtic teacher Pelagius, 'penetrate the thin veil that divides heaven from earth.'

The 1400th anniversary of Columba's death in 1997 further developed an awareness in Britain of Iona as one of the greatest centres of the ancient Celtic mission. Ironically 597 was also when Augustine of Canterbury began his mission from Rome, in exactly the same year as Columba's death. The Iona mission and the mission from Rome represented radically different ways of seeing. Two major features of the Celtic tradition distinguish it from what in contrast can be called the 'Mediterranean' tradition. Celtic spirituality is marked by the belief that what is deepest in us is the image of God. Sin has distorted and obscured that image but not erased it. The Mediterranean tradition, on the other hand, in its doctrine of original sin has taught that what is deepest in us is our sinfulness. This has given rise to a tendency to define ourselves in terms of the ugliness of our sin instead of the beauty of our origins. The second major characteristic of the Celtic tradition is a belief in the essential goodness of creation. Not only is creation viewed as a blessing, it is regarded as a theophany or a showing of God. Thus the great Celtic teachers refer to it as 'the book of creation' in which we may read the mystery of God. The Mediterranean tradition, on the other hand, has tended towards a separation of spirit and matter, and thus has distanced the mystery of God from the matter of creation.

The clash of these two traditions in Britain late in the 6th century led eventually to the Synod of Whitby in 664 and the tragic displacement of the Celtic mission. Banished to the edges of British Christianity the Celtic way of seeing was marginalised. Its spirituality was now to live on not within the four walls of organised religion but outwith the formal teachings and practices of the church, primarily on the Celtic fringes of Britain.

In my book *Listening for the Heartbeat of God* (1997) I outline the main characteristics of Celtic spirituality over the centuries and describe how it continued almost as a spiritual resistance movement in the Western Isles of Scotland. For hundreds of years the prayers of this spirituality were passed down in the oral tradition among men and women of Iona and the other islands. Many of these finally were collected and transcribed in the 19th century by a man named Alexander Carmichael. His six-volume work, entitled *Carmina Gadelica*, meaning 'Songs of the Gaels', conveys the distinct way of seeing expressed by the people of the islands in their prayers at the rising of the sun and at its setting, or at the kindling of the morning fire and at its 'smooring' or covering at night. These prayers, usually chanted or sung, were not uttered in religious contexts but rather were the songs of daily life. Again and again the perspective that comes across in the Celtic tradition is that the world is the temple of God. It is there that we join our voices to the ongoing song and rhythm of creation.

The prayers that Carmichael collected celebrate the essential goodness of all created life while at the same time being aware of suffering and evil. It is important not to romanticise this tradition for it was forged in the often inhospitable conditions of the west coast of Scotland. When crops failed there was terrible hardship, and in the fishing trade at sea many lives were lost. In addition to the harshness of the elements, the people of this tradition also increasingly faced the opposition, and sometimes the persecution, of the religion of the land. Viewed unsympathetically by outsiders, the sun and moon prayers, for instance, were regarded as pre-Christian and pantheistic. Especially from the 17th century onwards ministers and school teachers forbade the use of these prayers in their parishes.

By the time Carmichael made his collection in the 19th century, there were accounts not only of school children being beaten for singing these songs in the Gaelic but of ministers collecting and burning the fiddles and pipes of the people to prevent them from continuing the old songs and music. The greatest blow to their continued use were the Highland Clearances in the first half of the 19th century. Thousands of families were cleared from their ancestral lands and dispersed either to North America or to the streets of Glasgow. Torn apart from one another and from the crofting communities in which they had learned these prayers, the tradition began to falter and within a generation or two had largely been lost. If Carmichael had not made his collection from the old men and women, many of whom now wandered homelessly in the islands and highlands, this rich stream of prayer soon would have been erased from living memory.

The more I learned of the *Carmina Gadelica* tradition the more I came to see that this stream of spirituality is like a rich treasure trove from which we can draw today. I saw that these ancient prayers could be adapted for use in the Iona Community's weekly cycle of prayer. Christ is seen as being with and for the poor; healing is regarded as a grace that releases the essential well-being of nature; creation is viewed sacramentally; Christ is portrayed as liberator of the image of God at the core of our being; the life of heaven and the life of earth are viewed as bound together inextricably; and the delights and demands of welcome and hospitality – expecting to meet Christ in the stranger's guise – are accentuated. The prayers of this book are new expressions of the old words and imagery of Carmichael's great collection.

The rebirth of interest in things Celtic is widespread in the western world. My hope in continuing to offer these prayers is that, in addition to reading about our Celtic past or learning more of Celtic art and song, we may allow these rich and simple utterances of prayer to open in us new ways of seeing for today.

During my time at the Abbey the Iona Community generously provided me with a sabbatical and I used the time in part to work on the first edition of this book. I trust that it will continue to be of help to some of us, some of the time, in our prayers of wonder and hope for the world.

J. Philip Newell
Edinburgh

To my Mother and Father,
who taught me to pray

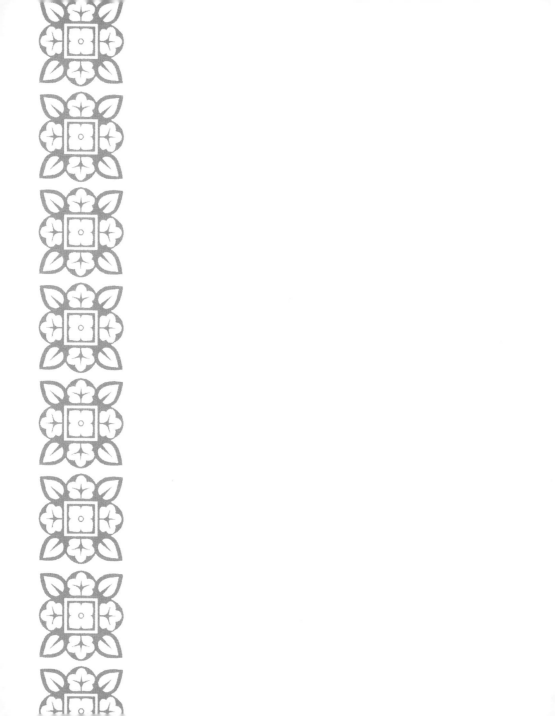

The Lord's Prayer

Our Father in heaven
Hallowed be your name
Your kingdom come
Your will be done
on earth as in heaven
Give us today our daily bread
Forgive us our sins
as we forgive those who sin against us
Lead us not into temptation
But deliver us from evil
For the kingdom, the power
and the glory are yours
Now and for ever
Amen.

MONDAY

Justice and Peace

You have searched me
and known me, O God.
You know when I sit down
and when I rise up.

(Ps 139:1–2)

Silence

*Be still
and aware of God's presence
within and all around.*

Opening prayer and thanksgiving

Thanks be to you, O God,
that I have risen this day
to the rising of this life itself.
May it be a day of blessing,
O God of every gift,
a day of new beginnings given.
Help me to avoid every sin
and the source of every sin to forsake,
and as the mist scatters
from the crest of the hills
may each ill haze clear
from my soul, O God.

Free prayers of thanks

The Lord's prayer

Scripture readings

(see appendix for psalms and gospels)

Silence

Reflect on the gospel
and remember
that God is with those
who are poor and betrayed.

Intercessions

O Christ of the poor and the yearning,
kindle in my heart within
a flame of love for my neighbour,
for my foe, for my friend,
for my kindred all.
From the humblest thing that lives
to the Name that is highest of all,
kindle in my heart within
a flame of love.

*Pray for the coming day
and for justice and peace.*

Closing prayer

This day and this night, O God,
may I know
the deep peace
of the running wave
the deep peace
of the flowing air
the deep peace
of the quiet earth
the deep peace
of the shining stars
the deep peace
of the Son of Peace.

You discern my thoughts
from far away, O God.
You search out my path
and my lying down
and are acquainted
with all my ways.

(Ps 139:2–3)

Silence

Be still
and aware of God's presence
within and all around.

Opening prayer and thanksgiving

O Christ of the least
and the homeless,
O Christ of the lost
and betrayed,
come close to me this night
that I may come close to you.
As you watched me with care
at my soul's shaping
look on me now with grace.
As you blessed me with light
at the sun's rising
shine on me now with love.

Free prayers of thanks

The Lord's Prayer

Scripture readings

Silence

Reflect on the gospel
and remember
that God is with those
who are poor and betrayed.

Intercessions

Peace between nations
peace between neighbours
peace between lovers
in love of the God of life.
Peace between man and woman
peace between parent and child
peace between brother and sister
the peace of Christ above all peace.
Bless O Christ my face,
let my face bless everything.
Bless O Christ my eyes,
let my eyes bless all they see.

*Recall the events of the day
and pray for justice and peace.*

Closing prayer

I end this day
as the Son of Mary would end it.
The grace of God be on this place
and on all whom
God has given me.
Who keeps watch
over us this night?
Who but the Christ of love.

TUESDAY

Prayers for Healing

If I ascend to heaven
you are there, O God.
And if I make my bed in hell,
still you are with me.

(Ps 139:8)

Silence

*Be still
and aware of God's presence
within and all around.*

Opening prayer and thanksgiving

In the beginning, O God,
you shaped my soul and set its weave.
You formed my body
and gave it breath.
Renew me this day
in the image of your love.
O great God, grant me your light.
O great God, grant me your grace.
O great God, grant me your joy this day
and let me be made pure
in the well of your health.

Free prayers of thanks

The Lord's Prayer

Scripture readings

Silence

Reflect on the gospel
and on the Christ of the cross,
suffering in the world
with all those who are broken.

Intercessions

O Christ of the road
of the wounded,
O Christ of the tears
of the broken,
in me and with me
the needs of the world.
Grant me my prayers
of loving and hoping.
Grant me my prayers
of yearning for healing.

Pray for the coming day
and for healing
within and among all people.

Closing prayer

God before me, God behind me,
God above me, God beneath me.
I on your path, O God,
you, O God, on my way.
In the twistings of the road
in the currents of the river
be with me by day
be with me by night
be with me by day and by night.

You are behind me
and before me, O God.
You lay your hand
upon me.

(Ps 139:5)

Silence

Be still
and aware of God's presence
within and all around.

Opening prayer and thanksgiving

As I utter these prayers
from my mouth, O God,
in my soul may I feel your presence.
The knee that is stiff
O healer make pliant.
The heart that is hard
make warm beneath your wing.
The wound that is giving me pain
O best of healers make whole.
And may my hopes and my fears
find a listening place with you.

Free prayers of thanks

The Lord's Prayer

Scripture readings

Silence

Reflect on the gospel
and on the Christ of the cross,
suffering in the world
with all those who are broken.

Intercessions

O God of the stars
and the night skies,
may your light be coming through
thick clouds this night,
on me and on everyone,
coming through dark tears,
on each one in need
and in suffering.

Recall the events of the day
and pray for healing
within and among all people.

Closing prayer

Christ stands before me
and peace is in his mind.
Sleep, O sleep
in the calm of all calm.
Sleep, O sleep
in the love of all loves.
Sleep I this night
in the God of all life.

WEDNESDAY

The Goodness of Creation
& Care for the Earth

It was you who formed
my inward parts,
you knit me together
in my mother's womb.
I praise you
for I am fearfully
and wonderfully made.

(Ps 139:13–14)

Silence

Be still
and aware of God's presence
within and all around.

Opening prayer and thanksgiving

O Sun behind all suns,
I give you greeting this new day.
Let all creation praise you.
Let the daylight
and the shadows praise you.
Let the fertile earth
and the swelling sea praise you.
Let the wind and the rain
the lightning and the thunder
praise you
Let all that breathes,
both male and female, praise you.
And I shall praise you.
O God of all life
I give you greeting this day.

Free prayers of thanks

The Lord's Prayer

Scripture readings

Silence

Reflect on the gospel
and on God
as the wellspring of all life.

Intercessions

There is no plant in the ground
but tells of your beauty, O Christ.
There is no creature on the earth,
there is no life in the sea
but proclaims your goodness.
There is no bird on the wing,
there is no star in the sky,
there is nothing beneath the sun
but is full of your blessing.
Lighten my understanding
of your presence all around, O Christ.
Kindle my will
to be caring for creation.

Pray for the coming day
and for the care of the earth.

Closing prayer

Bless to me, O God,
my soul that comes from on high.
Bless to me, O God,
my body that is of earth.
Bless to me, O God,
each thing my eye sees,
each sound my ear hears.
Bless to me, O God,
each scent that goes to my nostrils,
each taste that goes to my lips,
each ray that guides my way.

My frame
was not hidden from you
when I was being made
in secret,
intricately woven
in the depths of the earth.
Your eyes beheld
my unformed substance.

(Ps 139:15)

Silence

Be still
and aware of God's presence
within and all around.

Opening prayer and thanksgiving

You are the love
of each living creature, O God.
You are the warmth
of the rising sun.
You are the whiteness
of the moon at night.
You are the life
of the growing earth.
You are the strength
of the waves of the sea.
Speak to me this night, O God,
speak to me your truth.
Dwell with me this night, O God,
dwell with me in love.

Free prayers of thanks

The Lord's Prayer

Scripture readings

Silence

*Reflect on the gospel
and on God
as the wellspring of all life.*

Intercessions

You are above me, O God,
you are beneath.
You are in air,
you are in earth.
You are beside me,
you are within.
O God of heaven,
you have made your home on earth
in the broken body of creation.
Kindle within me
a love for you in all things.

Recall the events of the day
and pray for the care of the earth.

Closing prayer

May the grace of the love
of the stars be mine.
May the grace of the love
of the winds be mine.
May the grace of the love
of the waters be mine,
in the name of the Word
of all life.

THURSDAY

Commitment to Christ

If I take the wings
of the morning
and settle at
the furthest limits of the sea,
even there your hand
shall lead me
and your right hand
shall hold me fast.

(Ps 139:9–10)

Silence

*Be still
and aware of God's presence
within and all around.*

Opening prayer and thanksgiving

O loving Christ
who died upon the tree,
each day and each night
I remember your love.
In my lying down
and in my rising up,
in life and in death
you are my health and my peace.
Each day and each night
I remember your forgiveness
bestowed on me so gently
and generously.
Each day and each night
may I be fuller in love to you.

Free prayers of thanks

The Lord's Prayer

Scripture readings

Silence

Reflect on the gospel
and on the One who calls us
to follow him
as the way, the truth and the life.

Intercessions

Life be in my speech,
truth in what I say.
The love Christ Jesus gave
be filling every heart for me.
The love Christ Jesus gave
be filling me for everyone.

*Pray for the coming day
and to follow Christ more closely.*

Closing prayer

Bless to me, O God,
the earth beneath my feet.
Bless to me, O God,
the path on which I go.
Bless to me, O God,
the people whom I meet.
O God of all gods
bless to me my life.

If I say,
'Surely the darkness
shall cover me
and the light around me
become night',
even the darkness
is not dark to you.
The night is as bright
as the day, for darkness is as light to you.

(Ps 139:11–12)

Silence

*Be still
and aware of God's presence
within and all around.*

Opening prayer and thanksgiving

I am bending my knee
in the eye of the God
who created me,
in the eye of the Son
who died for me,
in the eye of the Spirit
who moves me
in love and in desire.
For the many gifts
you have bestowed on me
each day and night
each sea and land
each weather fair
each calm, each wild
thanks be to you, O God.

Free prayers of thanks

The Lord's Prayer

Scripture readings

Silence

Reflect on the gospel
and on the One who calls us to follow him
as the way, the truth and the life.

Intercessions

O God, I place myself
with those who struggle
this night.
I am here in need.
I am here in pain.
I am here alone.
O God, help me.

*Recall the events of the day
and pray for those who suffer.*

Closing prayer

O Christ, you are a bright flame before me.
You are a guiding star above me.
You are the light and love
I see in others' eyes.
Keep me, O Christ,
in a love that is tender.
Keep me, O Christ,
in a love that is true.
Keep me, O Christ,
in a love that is strong,
tonight, tomorrow and always.

FRIDAY

The Communion of Heaven & Earth

Where can I go
from your spirit, O God?

(Ps 139:7)

Silence

*Be still
and aware of God's presence
within and all around.*

Opening prayer and thanksgiving

I awake this morning in the presence
of the holy angels of God.
May heaven open wide before me
above me and around me
that I may see
the Christ of my love
and his sunlit company
in all things of earth this day.

Free prayers of thanks

The Lord's Prayer

Scripture readings

Silence

*Reflect on the gospel and remember
that the life of heaven
and the life of earth
are interwoven.*

Intercessions

O God of life, of all life, of each life,
I offer you my prayers
in the love of Christ
in the affection of Christ
in the company of Christ.
As your own household
desires in heaven
so may I desire on earth this day.

Pray for the coming day
and for the life of the world.

Closing prayer

The love and affection
of the angels be with me.
The love and affection
of the saints be with me.
The love and affection
of heaven be with me,
to lead me and to cherish me
this day.

Where can I flee
from your presence, O God?

(Ps 139:7)

Silence

Be still
and aware of God's presence
within and all around.

Opening prayer and thanksgiving

My Christ, my love,
my encircler,
each day, each night,
each light, each dark,
be near me, uphold me,
my treasure, my truth.

Free prayers of thanks

The Lord's Prayer

Scripture readings

Silence

Reflect on the gospel and remember
that the life of heaven
and the life of earth
are interwoven.

Intercessions

Safeguard your faithful people
in the sanctuary of your love, O God.
Shelter them this night
in the shelter of the saints.
God to enfold them
God to surround them
God in their watching
God in their hoping
God in their sleeping
God in their ever-living souls.

*Recall the events of the day
and pray for the life of the world.*

Closing prayer

Grant to me, O Trinity of grace
from whom all life freely flows,
that no tie over-strict
no tie over-dear
may be between myself
and this world.
As it was
as it is
as it shall be evermore,
with the ebb
with the flow
O Trinity of grace.

SATURDAY

Welcome & Hospitality

How weighty to me
are your thoughts, O God,
how vast is the sum of them.
If I should count them
they are more than the sand.
When I awake
I am still with you.

(Ps 139:17–18)

Silence

*Be still
and aware of God's presence
within and all around.*

Opening prayer and thanksgiving

O God who brought me
from the rest of last night
to the new light of this day,
bring me in the new light
of this day
to the guiding light
of the eternal.
Lead me, O God,
on the journey of justice.
Guide me, O God,
on the pathways of peace.
Renew me, O God,
by the wellsprings of grace,
today, tonight and for ever.

Free prayers of thanks

The Lord's Prayer

Scripture readings

Silence

Reflect on the gospel
and remember
Jesus identifying himself
with the homeless and rejected.

Intercessions

May those without shelter
be under your guarding
this day, O Christ.
May the wandering
find places of welcome.
O son of the tears, of the wounds,
of the piercings,
may your cross this day
be shielding them.

Pray for the coming day
and for those
without a place of welcome.

Closing prayer

On my heart and on my house
the blessing of God.
In my coming and in my going
the peace of God.
In my life and in my seeking
the love of God.
At my end and new beginning
the arms of God to welcome me
and bring me home.

Search me, O God,
and know my heart.
Test me and know my thoughts.
See if there is
any wicked way in me
and lead me
in the way everlasting.

(Ps 139:23–24)

Silence

Be still
and aware of God's presence
within and all around.

Opening prayer and thanksgiving

A shade are you in the heat, O God,
a shelter are you in the cold.
Eyes are you to the blind, O God,
a staff are you to the weak.
An island are you at sea, O God,
a rock are you on land.
O my soul's healer,
keep me at evening
keep me at morning
keep me at noon.
I am tired, astray and stumbling,
shield me from sin.
O my soul's healer,
shield me from sin.

Free prayers of thanks

The Lord's Prayer

Scripture readings

Silence

Reflect on the gospel
and remember
Jesus identifying himself
with the homeless and rejected.

Intercessions

Watch now, O Christ,
with those who are weary
or wandering
or weeping this night.
Guide them to a house
of your peace
and lead me to be caring
for their tears.

Recall the events of the day
and pray for those
without a place of welcome.

Closing prayer

I lie down this night with God
and God will lie down with me.
I lie down this night with Christ
and Christ will lie down with me.
I lie down this night with the Spirit
and the Spirit will lie down with me.
The Three of my love
will be lying down with me.
I shall not lie down with sin
nor shall sin or sin's shadow
lie down with me.
I lie down this night with God
and God will lie down with me.

A Weekday

LECTIONARY

of Psalms & Gospel Readings

A lectionary is simply a list of Scripture readings. These are selected for use throughout the Church's year, which begins not on January 1st but with Advent, four weeks before Christmas.

Christmastide is followed by the seasons of Epiphany and Lent. Ash Wednesday marks the beginning of Lent and is a preparation for the season of Easter. After the weeks of Easter, the long season of Pentecost begins and finally takes us back to Advent.

The key to using a lectionary is the calendar of movable feasts. Unlike Christmas, which always falls on the same date, other major feast days, such as Easter and Pentecost, change in date from year to year. This means that in following the lectionary it is also necessary to keep an eye on the calendar of movable feasts. There are notes throughout the lectionary to indicate when the calendar of movable feasts should be checked as a guide.

CALENDAR OF MOVABLE FEASTS

Year	Ash Wednesday	Easter	Ascension	Pentecost	First Sunday of Advent
2008	6 February	23 March	1 May	11 May	30 November
2009	25 February	12 April	21 May	31 May	29 November
2010	17 February	4 April	13 May	23 May	28 November
2011	9 March	24 April	2 June	12 June	27 November
2012	22 February	8 April	17 May	27 May	2 December
2013	13 February	31 March	9 May	19 May	1 December
2014	5 March	20 April	29 May	8 June	30 November
2015	18 February	5 April	14 May	24 May	29 November
2016	10 February	27 March	5 May	15 May	27 November
2017	1 March	16 April	25 May	4 June	3 December
2018	14 February	1 April	10 May	20 May	2 December
2019	6 March	21 April	30 May	9 June	1 December
2020	26 February	12 April	21 May	31 May	29 November

ADVENT

Advent 1
Week following Advent Sunday –
see calendar of movable feasts.
Mon   Ps 51, Matt 8:5–13
Tues   Ps 57, Luke 10:21–24
Wed   Ps 62, Matt 15:29–39
Thurs   Ps 65, Matt 7:21–27
Fri   Ps 67, Matt 9:27–31
Sat   Ps 75, Matt 9:35–38

Advent 2
Mon   Ps 77, Luke 5:17–26
Tues   Ps 80, Matt 18:10–14
Wed   Ps 82, Matt 11:25–30
Thurs   Ps 84, Matt 11:11–15
Fri   Ps 85, Matt 11:16–19
Sat   Ps 86, Matt 17:10–13

Advent 3
Mon   Ps 90, Matt 21:23–27
Tues   Ps 93, Matt 21:28–32
Wed   Ps 95, Luke 7:18–23
Thurs   Ps 96, Luke 7:24–35
Fri   Ps 98, John 5:30–36
Sat   Ps 99, Matt 1:1–17

Advent 4
If any of the days in Advent 4
fall on 24 December, go to the
Christmastide readings.
Mon   Ps 100, Matt 1:18–24
Tues   Ps 102, Luke 1:5–25

Wed   Ps 103, Luke 1:26–38
Thurs   Ps 104:1–34, Luke 1:39–45
Fri   Ps 107, Luke 1:46–56
Sat   Ps 111, Luke 1:57–66

CHRISTMASTIDE

Christmas Eve
24 Dec   Ps 113, Luke 1:67–79

Christmas Day
25 Dec   Ps 19, John 1:1–18

Feast of St Stephen
26 Dec   Ps 46, John 15:20–16.4

Feast of St John
27 Dec   Ps 103, John 13:21–35

Holy Innocents Day
28 Dec   Ps 128, Matt 18:1–10

29 Dec   Ps 133 and 134
           John 12:20–33
30 Dec   Ps 139:1–18
           John 12:34–50
31 Dec   Ps 147, Luke 21:25–36
1 Jan   Ps 148, Luke 2:21–40
2 Jan   Ps 146, John 1:19–28
3 Jan   Ps 150, John 1:29–34
4 Jan   Ps 6, John 1:35–42
5 Jan   Ps 113, John 1:43–51

EPIPHANY

Days at the beginning of Epiphany
Feast of Epiphany falls on 6 Jan
6 January   Ps 8, Matt 2:1–12
7 January   Ps 96, John 2:1–12 *
8 January   Ps 13, Matt 6:24–34 *
9 January   Ps 98, Mark 6:45–52 *
10 January   Ps 19, Luke 4:14–30 *
11 January   Ps 23, Luke 5:12–16 *
12 January   Ps 24, John 3:22–30 *
* If this day is a Monday go to the readings in the week Epiphany 1 below.

Epiphany 1
First full week after 6 January
Mon   Ps 27, Mark 1:14–20
Tues   Ps 30, Mark 1:21–28
Wed   Ps 33, Mark 1:29–39
Thurs   Ps 46, Mark 1:40–45
Fri   Ps 29, Mark 2:1–12
Sat   Ps 85, Mark 2:13–17

Epiphany 2
Mon   Ps 121, Mark 2:18–22
Tues   Ps 42, Mark 2:23–28
Wed   Ps 126, Mark 3:1–6
Thurs   Ps 50, Mark 3:7–12
Fri   Ps 51, Mark 3:13–19
Sat   Ps 67, Mark 3:20–30

Epiphany 3
Mon   Ps 57, Mark 3:31–35
Tues   Ps 62, Mark 4:1–9

Wed   Ps 65, Mark 4:10–20
Thurs   Ps 85, Mark 4:21–25
Fri   Ps 86, Mark 4:26–34
Sat   Ps 96, Mark 4:35–41

Epiphany 4
Mon   Ps 77, Mark 5:1–20
Tues   Ps 99, Mark 5:21–43
Wed   Ps 80, Mark 6:1–6
Thurs   Ps 82, Mark 6:7–13
Fri   Ps 84, Mark 6:14–29
Sat   Ps 100, Mark 6:30–44

Epiphany 5
Mon   Ps 90, Mark 5:53–56
Tues   Ps 93, Mark 7:1–13
Wed   Ps 95, Mark 7:14–23
Thurs   Ps 98, Mark 7:24–30
Fri   Ps 102, Mark 7:31–37
Sat   Ps 103, Mark 8:1–10

Check the date of Ash Wednesday in the Calendar of movable feasts, and then go to the appropriate week before Lent or to the Monday before Ash Wednesday.

Third week before Lent
Mon   Ps 127, Mark 8:11–13
Tues   Ps 128, Mark 8:14–21
Wed   Ps 107, Mark 8:22–26
Thurs   Ps 126, Mark 8:27–33
Fri   Ps 111, Mark 8:34–38
Sat   Ps 114, Mark 9:1–13

Second week before Lent

Mon	Ps 6: Mark 9:14–29
Tues	Ps 8, Mark 9:30–37
Wed	Ps 133, Mark 9:38–41
Thurs	Ps 13, Mark 9:42–50
Fri	Ps 75, Mark 10:1–12
Sat	Ps 113, Mark 10:13–16

First week before Lent

Mon	Ps 20, Mark 10:17–27
Tues	Ps 23, Mark 10:28–31
Wed	Ps 116, Mark 10:32–45
Thurs	Ps 118, Mark 10:46–52
Fri	Ps 139:1-18, Mark 11:11–26
Sat	Ps 24, Mark 11:27–33

LENT

Week in which Lent begins

Mon	Ps 57, Mark 12:1–12
Tues	Ps 103, Mark 12:13–17

Ash Wednesday

Wed	Ps 102, Matt 6:1–21
Thurs	Ps 42, Luke 9:18–27
Fri	Ps 43, Matt 9:14–17
Sat	Ps 46, Luke 5:27–32

Lent 1

Mon	Ps 51, Matt: 25:31–46
Tues	Ps 50, Luke 11:1–13
Wed	Ps 139:1-18, Luke 11:29–32
Thurs	Ps 62, Matt 7:7–12
Fri	Ps 65, Matt 5:21–26
Sat	Ps 67, Matt 5:43–48

Lent 2

Mon	Ps 19, Luke 6:37–42
Tues	Ps 27, Matt 23:1–12
Wed	Ps 75, Matt 20:17–28
Thurs	Ps 77, Luke 16:19–31
Fri	Ps 30, Matt 21:33–46
Sat	Ps 80, Luke 15:11–32

Lent 3

Mon	Ps 82, Luke 4:16–30
Tues	Ps 84, Matt 18:21–35
Wed	Ps 86, Matt 5:17–20
Thurs	Ps 90, Luke 11:14–23
Fri	Ps 93, Mark 12:28–34
Sat	Ps 95, Luke 18:9–14

Lent 4

Mon	Ps 99, John 4:43–54
Tues	Ps 103, John 5:1–18
Wed	Ps 104, John 5:19–29
Thurs	Ps 107, John 5:30–47
Fri	Ps 111, John 7:1–24
Sat	Ps 113, John 7:25–30

Lent 5

Mon	Ps 114, John 8:1–11
Tues	Ps 116, John 8:21–30
Wed	Ps 118, John 8:31–47
Thurs	Ps 121, John 8:48–59
Fri	Ps 123, John 10:22–42
Sat	Ps 43, John 11:45–57

Holy Week

Mon	Ps 25, John 12:1–11
Tues	Ps 27, John 12:37–50
Wed	Ps 22, John 13:21–35
Thurs	Ps 42, John 13:1–15
Fri	Ps 130, John 18:1–19:37
Sat	Ps 116, John 19:38–42

EASTER

Easter Week

Easter Day

Sun	Ps 113, John 20:1–18
Mon	Ps 122, Matt 28:11–15
Tues	Ps 124, John 20:19–29
Wed	Ps 127, Luke 24:13–35
Thurs	Ps 133, 134, Luke 24:36–49
Fri	Ps 138, John 21:1–14
Sat	Ps 139:1–18, Mark 16:9–18

Easter 1

Mon	Ps 146, John 3:1–8
Tues	Ps 147, John 3:9–13
Wed	Ps 148, John 3:14–21
Thurs	Ps 150, John 3:31–36
Fri	Ps 46, John 6:1–15
Sat	Ps 29, John 6:16–21

Easter 2

Mon	Ps 8, John 6:22–29
Tues	Ps 13, John 6:30–35
Wed	Ps 16, John 6:35–40
Thurs	Ps 19, John 6:44–51
Fri	Ps 20, John 6:53–59
Sat	Ps 23, John 6:60–69

Easter 3

Mon	Ps 24, John 10:10–8
Tues	Ps 25, John 10:9–18
Wed	Ps 27, John 12:44–50
Thurs	Ps 29, John 13:16–20
Fri	Ps 30, John 14:1–6
Sat	Ps 33, John 14:7–14

Easter 4

Mon	Ps 42, John 14:21–26
Tues	Ps 43, John 14:27–31
Wed	Ps 46, John 15:1–8
Thurs	Ps 50, John 15:9–11
Fri	Ps 51, John 15:12–17
Sat	Ps 57, John 15:18–21

Easter 5

Mon	Ps 62, John 15:26–16:4
Tues	Ps 65, John 16:5–11
Wed	Ps 67, John 16:12–15
Ascension Day	
Thurs	Ps 96, Luke 24:44–53
Fri	Ps 75, John 16:20–23
Sat	Ps 77, John 16:24–28

Easter 6

Mon	Ps 121, John 16:29–33
Tues	Ps 126, John 17:1–11
Wed	Ps 138, John 17:12–19
Thurs	Ps 150, John 17:20–26
Fri	Ps 80, John 21:15–19
Sat	Ps 104:1–34, John 21:20–25

PENTECOST

The season of Pentecost can begin as early as 10 May and as late as 13 June. See the date of Pentecost in the calendar of movable feasts and go to the appropriate week.

Week beginning Sun 8–14 May
Mon	Ps 82, Matt 5:1–12
Tues	Ps 84, Matt 5:13–16
Wed	Ps 85, Matt 5:17–20
Thurs	Ps 86, Matt 5:21–26
Fri	Ps 90, Matt 5:27–32
Sat	Ps 93, Matt 5:33–37

Week beginning 15–21 May
Mon	Ps 95, Matt 5:38–42
Tues	Ps 96, Matt 5:43–48
Wed	Ps 98, Matt 6:1–6
Thurs	Ps 99, Matt 6:7–15
Fri	Ps 100, Matt 6:16–18
Sat	Ps 102, Matt 6:19–23

Week beginning 22–28 May
Mon	Ps 103, Matt 6:24–34
Tues	Ps 104:1–34, Matt 7:1–6
Wed	Ps 107, Matt 7:7–11
Thurs	Ps 111 Matt 7:12–14
Fri	Ps 113, Matt 7:15–20
Sat	Ps 114, Matt 7:21–29

Week beginning 29 May–4 June
Mon	Ps 116, Matt 8:1–4
Tues	Ps 118, Matt 8:5–13
Wed	Ps 121, Matt 8:14–17
Thurs	Ps 122, Matt 8:18–22
Fri	Ps 123, Matt 8:23–27
Sat	Ps 124, Matt 8:28–34

Week beginning 5–11 June
Mon	Ps 126, Matt 9:1–8
Tues	Ps 127, Matt 9:9–13
Wed	Ps 128, Matt 9:14–17
Thurs	Ps 130, Matt 9:18–26
Fri	Ps 133, 134, Matt 9:27–31
Sat	Ps 138, Matt 9:32–38

Week beginning 12–18 June
Mon	Ps 139:1–18, Matt 10:1–7
Tues	Ps 146, Matt 10:7–15
Wed	Ps 147, Matt 10:16–23
Thurs	Ps 148, Matt 10:24–33
Fri	Ps 150, Matt 10:34–39
Sat	Ps 6, Matt 10:40–42

Week beginning 19–25 June
Mon	Ps 8, Matt 11:1–6
Tues	Ps 13, Matt 11:7–15
Wed	Ps 16, Matt 11:16–19
Thurs	Ps 19, Matt 11:20–24
Fri	Ps 20, Matt 11:25–27
Sat	Ps 22, Matt 11:28–30

Week beginning 26 June–2 July

Mon	Ps 23, Matt 12:1–8
Tues	Ps 24, Matt 12:14–21
Wed	Ps 25, Matt 12:33–37
Thurs	Ps 27, Matt 12:38–42
Fri	Ps 29, Matt 12:43–45
Sat	Ps 30, Matt 12:46–50

Week beginning 3–9 July

Mon	Ps 33, Matt 13:1–9
Tues	Ps 42, Matt 13:10–17
Wed	Ps 43, Matt 13:18–21
Thurs	Ps 46, Matt 13:24–30
Fri	Ps 50, Matt 13:31–35
Sat	Ps 51, Matt 13:36–43

Week beginning 10–16 July

Mon	Ps 57, Matt 13:44–46
Tues	Ps 62, Matt 13:47–52
Wed	Ps 65, Matt 13:53–58
Thurs	Ps 67, Matt 14:1–12
Fri	Ps 75, Matt 14:13–21
Sat	Ps 77, Matt 14:22–36

Week beginning 17–23 July

Mon	Ps 80, Matt 15:1–9
Tues	Ps 82, Matt 15:10–20
Wed	Ps 84, Matt 15:21–28
Thurs	Ps 85, Matt 15:29–31
Fri	Ps 86, Matt 15:32–39
Sat	Ps 90, Matt 16:1–4

Week beginning 24–30 July

Mon	Ps 93, Matt 16:5–12
Tues	Ps 95, Matt 16:13–23
Wed	Ps 96, Matt 16:24–28
Thurs	Ps 98, Matt 17:1–8
Fri	Ps 99, Matt 17:14–21
Sat	Ps 100, Matt 17:22–27

Week beginning 31 July–6 August

Mon	Ps 102, Matt 18:1–14
Tues	Ps 103, Matt 18:15–20
Wed	Ps 104:1–34, Matt 18:21–35
Thurs	Ps 107, Matt 19:1–12
Fri	Ps 111, Matt 19:13–15
Sat	Ps 113, Matt 19:16–22

Week beginning 7–13 August

Mon	Ps 114, Matt 19:23–30
Tues	Ps 116, Matt 20:1–16
Wed	Ps 118, Matt 22:1–14
Thurs	Ps 121, Matt 22:34–40
Fri	Ps 122, Matt 23:1–12
Sat	Ps 123, Matt 23:13–22

Week beginning 14–20 August

Mon	Ps 124, Matt 23:23–26
Tues	Ps 126, Matt 23:27–32
Wed	Ps 127, Matt 24:42–51
Thurs	Ps 128, Matt 25:1–13
Fri	Ps 130, Matt 25:14–30
Sat	Ps 133, 134, Matt 25:31–40

Week beginning 21–27 August

Mon	Ps 138, Luke 4:16–30
Tues	Ps 139:1–18, Luke 4:31–37
Wed	Ps 146, Luke 4:38–41
Thurs	Ps 147, Luke 4:42–44
Fri	Ps 148, Luke 5:1–11
Sat	Ps 150, Luke 5:12–16

Week beginning 28 August–3 September

Mon	Ps 6, Luke 5:17–26
Tues	Ps 8, Luke 5:27–32
Wed	Ps 13, Luke 5:33–39
Thurs	Ps 16, Luke 6:1–5
Fri	Ps 19, Luke 6:6–11
Sat	Ps 20, Luke 6:12–19

Week beginning 4–10 September

Mon	Ps 22, Luke 6:20–26
Tues	Ps 23, Luke 6:27–31
Wed	Ps 24, Luke 6:32–36
Thurs	Ps 25, Luke 6:37–38
Fri	Ps 27, Luke 6:39–42
Sat	Ps 29, Luke 6:43–49

Week beginning 11–17 September

Mon	Ps 30, Luke 7:1–10
Tues	Ps 33, Luke 7:11–17
Wed	Ps 42, Luke 7:31–35
Thurs	Ps 43, Luke 7:36–50
Fri	Ps 46, Luke 8:1–3
Sat	Ps 50, Luke 8:4–15

Week beginning 18–24 September

Mon	Ps 51, Luke 8:16–18
Tues	Ps 57, Luke 8:19–21
Wed	Ps 62, Luke 9:1–6
Thurs	Ps 65, Luke 9:7–9
Fri	Ps 67, Luke 9:18–22
Sat	Ps 75, Luke 9:44–45

Week beginning 26 September–1 October

Mon	Ps 80, Luke 9:46–50
Tues	Ps 82, Luke 9:51–56
Wed	Ps 84, Luke 9:57–62
Thurs	Ps 85, Luke 10:1–12
Fri	Ps 86, Luke 10:13–16
Sat	Ps 90, Luke 10:17–24

Week beginning 2–8 October

Mon	Ps 93, Luke 10:25–37
Tues	Ps 95, Luke 10:38–42
Wed	Ps 96, Luke 11:1–4
Thurs	Ps 98, Luke 11:5–13
Fri	Ps 99, Luke 11:14–26
Sat	Ps 100, Luke 11:27–28

Week beginning 9–15 October

Mon	Ps 102, Luke 11:29–32
Tues	Ps 103, Luke 11:37–41
Wed	Ps 104:1–34, Luke 11:42–46
Thurs	Ps 107, Luke 11:47–54
Fri	Ps 111, Luke 12:1–7
Sat	Ps 113, Luke 12:8–12

Week beginning 16–22 October

Mon	Ps 114, Luke 12:13–21
Tues	Ps 116, Luke 12:35–40
Wed	Ps 118, Luke 12:41–48
Thurs	Ps 121, Luke 12:49–53
Fri	Ps 122, Luke 12:54–59
Sat	Ps 123, Luke 13:1–9

Week beginning 23–39 October

Mon	Ps 124, Luke 13:10–17
Tues	Ps 126, Luke 13:18–21
Wed	Ps 127, Luke 13:22–30
Thurs	Ps 128, Luke 13:31–35
Fri	Ps 130, Luke 14:1–6
Sat	Ps 133, 134, Luke 14:7–11

Week beginning 30 October–5 November

Mon	Ps 138, Luke 14:12–14
Tues	Ps 139:1–18, Luke 14:15–24
Wed	Ps 146, Luke 14:25–33
Thurs	Ps 147, Luke 15:1–10
Fri	Ps 148, Luke 16:1–8
Sat	Ps 150, Luke 16:9–15

Week beginning 6–12 November

Mon	Ps 6, Luke 17:1–6
Tues	Ps 8, Luke 17:7–10
Wed	Ps 13, Luke 17:11–19
Thurs	Ps 16, Luke 17:20–25
Fri	Ps 19, Luke 17:26–37
Sat	Ps 20, Luke 18:1–8

Week beginning 13–19 November

Mon	Ps 22, Luke 18:35–43
Tues	Ps 23, Luke 19:1–10
Wed	Ps 24, Luke 19:11–28
Thurs	Ps 25, Luke 19:41–44
Fri	Ps 27, Luke 19:45–58
Sat	Ps 29, Luke 20:27–40

Week before Advent

Mon	Ps 30, Luke 21:1–4
Tues	Ps 33, Luke 21:5–11
Wed	Ps 42, Luke 21:12–19
Thurs	Ps 43, Luke 21:20–28
Fri	Ps 46, Luke 21:29–33
Sat	Ps 50, Luke 21:34–38

THE IONA COMMUNITY

The Iona Community, founded in 1938 by the Revd George MacLeod, then a parish minister in Glasgow, is an ecumenical Christian community committed to seeking new ways of living the Gospel in today's world. Initially working to restore part of the medieval abbey on Iona, the Community today remains committed to 'rebuilding the common life' through working for social and political change, striving for the renewal of the church with an ecumenical emphasis, and exploring new, more inclusive approaches to worship, all based on an integrated understanding of spirituality.

The Community now has 280 Members, about 1500 Associate Members and around 1500 Friends. The Members – women and men from many denominations and backgrounds (lay and ordained), living throughout Britain with a few overseas – are committed to a fivefold Rule of devotional discipline, sharing and accounting for use of time and money, regular meeting, and action for justice and peace.

At the Community's three residential centres – the Abbey and the MacLeod Centre on Iona, and Camas Adventure Camp on the Ross of Mull – guests are welcomed from March to October and over Christmas. Hospitality is provided for over 110 people, along with a unique opportunity, usually through week-long programmes, to extend horizons and forge relationships through sharing an experience of the common life in worship, work, discussion and relaxation. The Community's shop on Iona, just outside the Abbey grounds, carries an attractive range of books and craft goods.

The Community's administrative headquarters are in Glasgow, which also serves as a base for its work with young people, the Wild Goose Resource Group working in the field of worship, a bi-monthly magazine, *Coracle*, and a publishing house, Wild Goose Publications.

For information on the Iona Community contact:
The Iona Community, Fourth Floor, Savoy House, 140 Sauchiehall Street,
Glasgow G2 3DH, UK. Phone: 0141 332 6343
e-mail: admin@iona.org.uk; web: www.iona.org.uk

For enquiries about visiting Iona, please contact:
Iona Abbey, Isle of Iona, Argyll PA76 6SN, UK. Phone: 01681 700404
e-mail: ionacomm@iona.org.uk

Also from Wild Goose Publications ...

RECLAIMING THE SEALSKIN
Meditations in the Celtic spirit
Annie Heppenstall-West

Seventy contemplations on the natural world and some human-made objects form the core of this book, which is inspired by the Celtic legend of the selkie, a mythical seal-like creature who could also live on the land in human form but sometimes became trapped because a human stole its sealskin. The selkie's vast nameless longing for the ocean is analogous to the soul's longing for the ocean of God.

In the spirit of modern Celtic Christianity, one of the purposes of this book is to discover parallels between traditional scripture and the contemplation of nature, and to harmonise the two. The author believes that the creatures and plants around us have a voice to help us in our search for the sealskin – our spiritual freedom.

Includes full-colour meditation cards that can be detached and used as an aid to contemplation.

192 pp   ISBN 1 901557 66 9

COLUMBA
Pilgrim and penitent
Ian Bradley

Examines the life, character and achievements of St Columba, and the distinctive nature and current relevance of Columban Christianity and its key strands – pilgrimage, penitence and politics. This saint's message has never been more timely than now, more than 1400 years after his death.

128 pp   ISBN 0 947988 81 5

To see more publications visit www.ionabooks.com

THIS IS THE DAY
Readings and meditations from the Iona Community
Neil Paynter

Daily readings for four months from a wide range of contributors within the Iona Community. These prayers, liturgies, songs, poems and articles, which reflect the concerns of the Community, can be used for group or individual reflection and are intended to inspire positive action and change in our lives. Subjects covered include: hospitality and welcome; prayer; justice and peace; the environment; healing; social action; church renewal; worship; work; racial justice; women; community; pilgrimage; sexuality; Columban Christianity and the Celtic tradition; ecumenism; inferfaith dialogue; nonviolence and peacekeeping; spirituality; commitment; economic witness; youth; liturgies.

320 pp   ISBN 1 901557 63 4

MAKER'S BLESSING
Iona Community

An elegant pocket-sized gift book of 48 pages containing a collection of inspirational prayers and meditations taken from previous Iona Community publications. With a hard cover.

48 pp   ISBN 1 901557 24 3